IR

Zoom In on
Our Renewable Earth

Water

Andrea Rivera

abdopublishing.com

Published by Abdo Zoom™, PO Box 398166, Minneapolis, Minnesota 55439. Copyright © 2017 by Abdo Consulting Group, Inc. International copyrights reserved in all countries. No part of this book may be reproduced in any form without written permission from the publisher. Abdo Zoom™ is a trademark and logo of Abdo Consulting Group, Inc.

Printed in the United States of America, North Mankato, Minnesota
102016
012017

THIS BOOK CONTAINS
RECYCLED MATERIALS

Cover Photo: Chepko Danil Vitalevich/Shutterstock Images
Interior Photos: Chepko Danil Vitalevich/Shutterstock Images, 1;
Borut Trdina/iStockphoto, 4–5; Valentyn Volkov/Shutterstock Images, 5;
Fabbio Lamanna/iStockphoto, 6–7; iStockphoto, 8–9, 17; Shutterstock Images, 10, 12, 15, 18;
Helen Hotson/Shutterstock Images, 11; Robert Kneschke/Shutterstock Images, 13;
Chamille White/Shutterstock Images, 14; Anibal Trejo/Shutterstock Images, 16;
Jordi Pratt Puig/Shutterstock Images, 19; Martin Wahlborg/iStockphoto, 21

Editor: Emily Temple
Series Designer: Madeline Berger
Art Direction: Dorothy Toth

Publisher's Cataloging-in-Publication Data
Names: Rivera, Andrea, author.
Title: Water / by Andrea Rivera.
Description: Minneapolis, MN : Abdo Zoom, 2017. | Series: Our renewable Earth |
    Includes bibliographical references and index.
Identifiers: LCCN 2016948928 | ISBN 9781680799422 (lib. bdg.) |
    ISBN 9781624025280 (ebook) | ISBN 9781624025846 (Read-to-me ebook)
Subjects: LCSH: Water conservation--Juvenile literature. | Conservation of natural
    resources--Juvenile literature. | Renewable energy sources--Juvenile literature.
Classification: DDC 333.91--dc23
LC record available at http://lccn.loc.gov/2016948928

Table of Contents

Water covers much of Earth's surface. Plants and animals need water to survive.

Water can be a solid,
liquid, or gas.

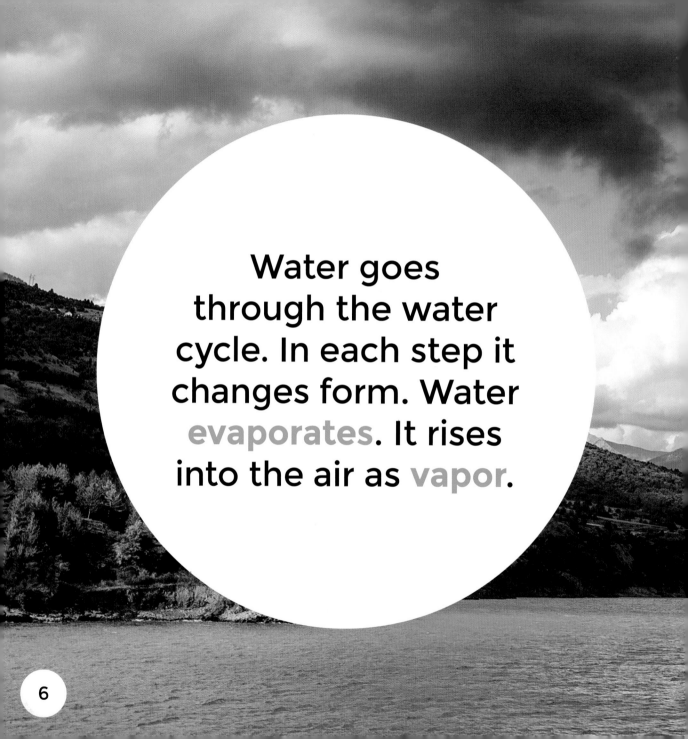

Water goes through the water cycle. In each step it changes form. Water **evaporates**. It rises into the air as **vapor**.

Vapor gathers together in a cloud. Then it falls to the ground as rain or snow.

Technology

Heating water changes it into a gas. It becomes steam.

Steam can be used to power an **engine**.

The steam spins a turbine.
This makes power.

Steam engines can power boats and trains.

Most water is
deep underground.

12

Plants soak up some of this water. Some seeps out to rivers or lakes.

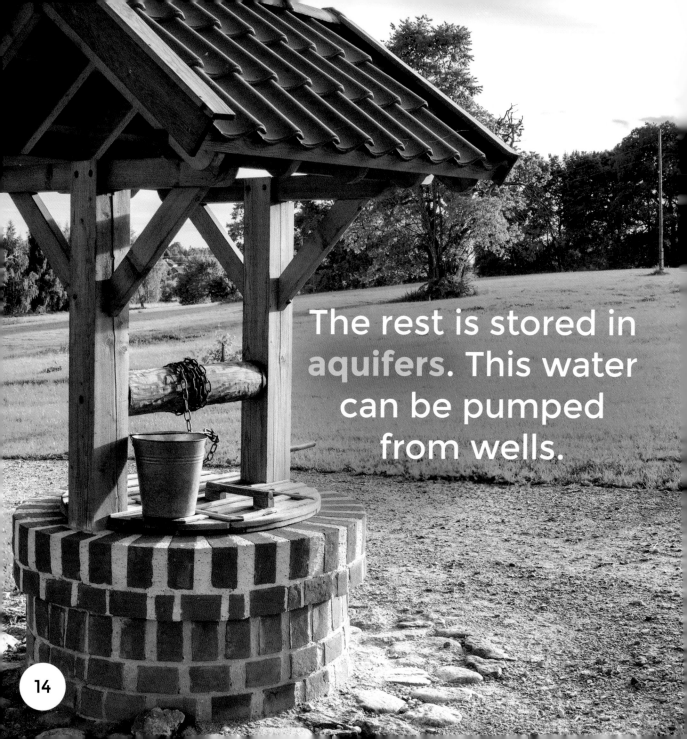

The rest is stored in **aquifers**. This water can be pumped from wells.

It comes to the surface
where it can be used.

Fountains shoot
water into the air.

Some have **sculptures**.
Others have colored lights.
A few fountains play music, too.

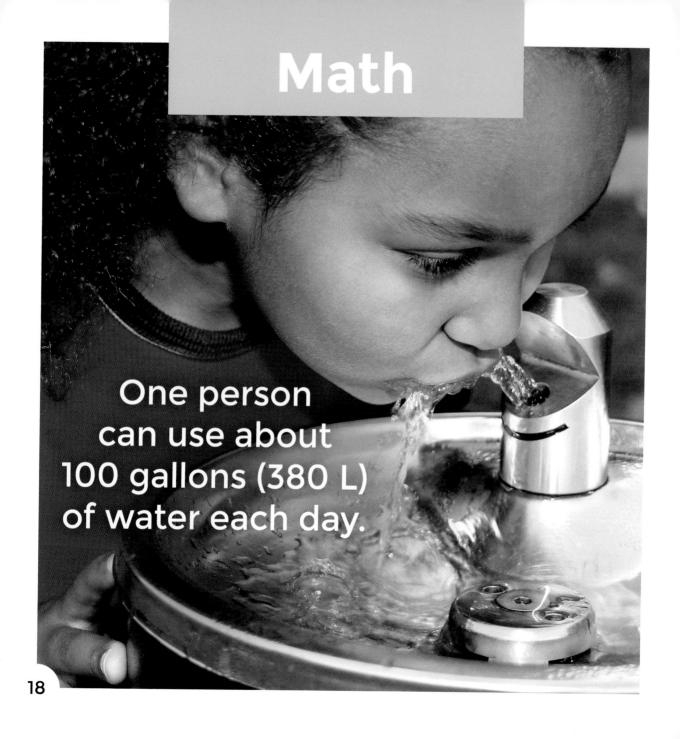

Math

One person can use about 100 gallons (380 L) of water each day.

That is 700 gallons (2,650 L) each week. Each minute of a shower uses about five gallons (19 L) of water.

Key Stats

- About two-thirds of a person's body is made of water.

- There are two kinds of water in the water cycle: saltwater and freshwater. Saltwater is in oceans.

- Only three percent of water on Earth is freshwater. Most rivers, streams, and lakes contain freshwater.

- There is 100 times more water underground than there is in all of Earth's lakes and rivers combined.

Glossary

aquifer - a layer of rock or sand that holds water.

engine - a machine that creates energy to make something work.

evaporates - changes from a liquid into a gas.

sculpture - an art form that is 3-D (not flat), like a statue.

turbine - an engine that includes blades. Air, steam, or water moves the blades.

vapor - water in gas form.

Booklinks

For more information
on water, please visit
booklinks.abdopublishing.com

Zoom In on STEAM!

Learn even more with the Abdo Zoom
STEAM database. Check out
abdozoom.com for more information.

Index